BELIEVE IN YOURSELF

Dr Joseph Murphy

The Milky Way Publications

ISBN: 978-81-973124-7-2

Publisher: The Milky Way Publications
Mumbai, Maharashtra

Phone: +91 9167080475
WhatsApp: +91 9167080475
E-mail: themilkywaypublications@gmail.com

First Edition: 2024

Believe in Yourself
Dr Joseph Murphy

About the Author

Dr. Murphy, Joseph (20 May 1898-16 Dec. 1981), religious leader and writer, was born Joseph Denis Murphy in County Cork, Ireland, the son of Denis Murphy, the head of a Jesuit boys school called the National School of Ireland, and Ellen Connolly. Denis Murphy was one of the few laymen to teach in a church school in Ireland and was a deacon in the Roman Catholic Church. Joseph grew up in a devout religious home, attending his father's school and preparing to study for the priesthood, but he began to have doubts about church doctrine in his late teens and withdrew from the seminary. At around this time he experienced the healing of a malignancy, a recovery that he attributed to personal prayer, and this proved a turning point in his spiritual life.

Determined to explore new ideas, he moved to the United States in 1922. When the United States entered World War I, he closed his successful business to join the army and served as a pharmacist in the medical unit of the 88th Infantry Division until 1918.

Murphy had been interested in religion since the medical recovery he associated with prayer, and while in the army he began to read about various faiths. When he returned to civilian life he abandoned pharmacology for travel and study, making trips to Europe and Asia to investigate other spiritual systems. In New York he began attending services at the Church of the Healing Christ, a part of the Church of Divine Science, one of the major denominations of the growing spiritual movement known as New Thought. An important influence on his thinking at this time was Thomas Troward (1847-1916), a British author whose books on spiritual metaphysics had a profound effect on the New Thought movement. Troward's involvement with

Freemasonry led Murphy to become active in the order, in whose ranks he was to reach the 32nd degree. In the mid1940s Murphy moved to Los Angeles, where he met Ernest Shurtleff Holmes (1887-1960), the founder of Religious Science, another branch of New Thought. This pioneer self-help writer, the author of the hugely successful book Creative Mind and Success (1919), guided Murphy to a fulltime study of Religious Science and in 1946 he was ordained a minister of that denomination and began teaching at its Institute of Religious Science.

He later met Erwin Gregg, the president of the Association of Divine Science and, drawn back to that faith, he was reordained to its ministry in 1949. He became the director of the Church of Divine Science in Los Angeles; soon it had the largest congregation of any of that denomination's churches in the United States, with lectures attended by 1,300 to 1,500 people every Sunday. He also broadcast a weekly radio program to an audience said to exceed a million listeners. His sermons, lectures, and radio broadcasts were so popular that he summarized them in church bulletins and, to reach a larger audience, began to record and sell cassette tapes of them. During that decade he returned to school, earning a Ph.D. in psychology from the University of Southern California.

Described by one of his publishers as "prosperity writer extraordinaire, Murphy made a direct appeal to his followers' ambitions for wealth. His How to Attract Money, originally published as a fifty-two-page pamphlet in 1957, asserts in its promotional literature, "It is your right to be rich. You are here to lead the abundant life, and to be happy, radiant, and free. You should therefore have all the money you need to lead a full, happy, prosperous life." Murphy later published Riches Are Your Right (1958) and Your Infinite Power to Be Rich (1966). His subject matter was not limited to financial success, however; his themes ranged widely across the spectrum of Eastern and Western thought, drawing from both his personal studies of Divine Science and Asian religions and his formal education in clinical psychology. He discussed personal relations (Love Is Freedom, 1948), emotional serenity (Peace within Yourself, 1956); Asian divination (Secrets of the "I Ching," 1970), and the paranormal (Psychic Perception: The Magic of Extrasensory Perception, 1971). Of all his more than thirty books, nothing he wrote was more successful than the selfhelp manual The Power of Your Subconscious Mind (1963), which promises in its introduction to "lift you up from confusion, misery, melancholy, and failure, and guide you to your true place, solve your difficulties, sever you from emotional and physical bondage, and place you on the royal road to freedom, happiness, and peace of mind" An instant best-seller, it sold more than ten million copies in twenty-six languages during its author's lifetime.

Contents

Chapter One
Make Your Dreams Come True

Joseph, in the Bible, means 'disciplined or controlled imagination. It is one of the primal faculties of mind.

It has the power to project and clothe your ideas, giving them visibility on the screen of space.

Israel loved Joseph. Israel is the spiritually awakened man who knows the power of controlled imagination. It is called the 'son of his old age. *Son* means 'expression.' *Old age* infers wisdom and knowledge of the laws of mind. When you become familiar with the power of imagination, you will call it 'the son of your old age.' *Age* is not the flight of years; it is really the dawn of wisdom and Divine knowledge in you. *Imagination* is the mighty instrument used by great scientists, artists, physicists, inventors, architects and mystics. When the world said, 'It *is* impossible; it can't be done, the man with imagination said, 'It is done! Through your imagination, you can also penetrate the depths of reality to reveal the secrets of nature.

A great industrialist told me one time how he started in a small store. He said that I used to dream (Joseph was a dreamer) of a large corporation with branches all over the country. He added that regularly, systematically he pictured in his mind the giant buildings. Offices, factories and stores, knowing that through the alchemy of the mind, he could weave the fabric out of which his dreams would be clothed.

He prospered, began to attract to himself—by a universal law of attraction—the ideas, personnel, friends, money, just everything needed for the emergence of his ideal. He truly exercised and cultivated his imagination. Now he lived with these mental patterns in his mind until imagination clothed them in form.

I particularly liked one comment that he made as follows: 'It is just as easy to imagine yourself successful, as it is to imagine failure but far more interesting.'

Joseph is a dreamer-a dreamer of dreams. This means he has visions, images and ideals in his mind and knows that there is a Creative Power that responds to his mental pictures. The mental images we hold are developed in feeling. It is wisely said that all our senses are modifications of the one-sense-feeling. Thomas Troward, a teacher of mental science, says, 'Feeling is the law and the law is the feelingFeeling is the fountainhead of power. We must charge our mental pictures with feeling in order to get results.

We are told, 'Joseph dreamed a dream. When he told it to his family they hated him. Perhaps as you read this, you have a dream, an ideal, a plan or purpose that you would like to accomplish. *To hate* is to reject in Bible language. The thoughts, feelings, beliefs and opinions in your mind are the brethren that challenge you, belittle your dreams and say to you, You can't; it is impossible. Forget it!

Perhaps other thoughts come into your mind, which scoff at your plan or ambition. You discover that there is a quarrel in your mind with your own society: opposition sets in. The way to handle the opposition in your mind is to detach your attention from evidence of only what you can see and hear that is, the appearance of things. You need to begin to think clearly and with interest about your goal or objective. When your mind is engaged on your goal or objective, you are using the creative law of mind—it will come to pass.

'Lo, my sheaf arose and also stood upright; and, behold, your sheaves stood round about and made obeisance to my sheaf.' (Genesis 37:7) Lift your ideal or desire up in consciousness. Exalt it. Commit yourself wholeheartedly to it. Praise it; give

your attention, love and devotion to your ideal; and as you continue to do so, all the fearful thoughts will make obeisance to your exalted state of mind—that is, they will lose their power and disappear from the mind.

Through your faculty to imagine the end result, you have control over any circumstance or condition. If you wish to bring about the realisation of any wish, desire or idea, form a mental picture of fulfillment in your mind; constantly imagine the reality of your desire. In this way, you will actually compel it into being. What you imagine as true already exists in the next dimension of your mind. If you remain faithful to your ideal, it will one day objectify itself. The master architect within you will project on the screen of visibility what you impress on your mind.

Joseph (imagination) wears a coat of many colors. A *coat* in the Bible is a psychological covering. Your psychological garments are the mental attitudes, moods and feelings you entertain. *The coat of many colors* represents the many facets of the diamond or your capacity to clothe any idea into reality. You can imagine your friend who is poor living in the lap of luxury. You can see his face light up with joy, see his expression change with a broad smile cross his lips. You can hear him tell you what you want to hear. You can see him exactly as you wish to see him—that is, he is radiant, happy, prosperous as also successful. Your imagination is the *coat of many colors*; it can clothe and objectify any idea or desire. You can imagine abundance where lack is, peace where discord is as well as health where there is sickness.

'His brethren said to him, "Shalt thou indeed reign over us?"' Imagination is the first faculty.It takes precedence over all the other powers or elements of consciousness. You have twelve faculties or brethren, but your imagination when disciplined enables you to collapse time and space and rise above all limitations. When you keep your imagination busy with noble,

Godlike concepts and ideas, you will find that it is the most effective of all faculties in your ongoing spiritual quest.

The phrase 'Joseph is sold into Egypt' means that your concept or desire must be subjectively understood (Egypt) first before it becomes objectified. Every concept must go 'down into Egypt,' meaning into the subjective space where the birth of ideas takes place.

'Out of Egypt have I called my son': Joseph is the commander of Egypt. This tells you that imagination controls the whole conceptive realm. Whatever prison you may be in, whether it is the prison of fear, sickness, lack or limitation of any kind, remember that Joseph is the commander in prison who can deliver you. You can imagine your freedom and continue to do so until it is subjectively understood; then, after gestation in the darkness, the manifestation comes—your prayer is answered.

Consider for a moment a distinguished, talented architect, who can build a beautiful, modern, 20th-century city in his mind—complete with super highways, swimming pools, aquariums, parks and so on. He can construct in his mind the most beautiful palace the eye has ever seen. He can see the building in its entirety completely erected before he ever gives his plan to the builders. Where was the building? It was in his imagination.

With *your* imagination, you can actually hear the invisible voice of your mother even though she lives 10,000 miles from here. You can also see her clearly, quite as vividly as if she were present. This is the wonderful power you possess. *You* can develop and cultivate this power to become successful and prosperous.

Haven't you heard the sales manager say, 'I have to let John go, because his attitude is wrong?' The business world knows the importance of 'right attitude.'

I remember many years ago having printed a small article on reincarnation. These pamphlets were on display on a book counter of a church where I lectured. In the beginning, very few of them were sold because the salesgirl was violently opposed to its contents.

I explained the Biblical meaning of reincarnation to her, the origin of the story as well as what it was all about. She understood the contents of the drama and became enthusiastic about the booklets; they were all sold before my lecture series was completed. This was an instance of the importance of the right mental attitude.

Your *mental attitude* means your mental reaction to people, circumstances, conditions and objects in space. What is your relationship with your co-workers? Are you friendly with people, with animals and with the universe in general? Do you think that the universe is hostile? Or that the world owes you a living? In short, what is your attitude?

The emotional reaction of the above-mentioned girl was one of deep-seated prejudice. That was the *wrong attitude* in selling books; she was biased toward the book and the writer.

You can develop the right mental attitude when you realize that nothing externally can upset you or hurt you without your mental consent. You are the only thinker in your world; consequently, nothing can move you to anger, grief or sorrow without your mental consent. The suggestions that come to you from the outside have no power whatsoever, except that you permit them to move you in thought negatively. Realize that you are master of your thought-world. Emotions follow thought; hence, you are supreme in your own orbit. Do you permit others to influence you? Do you allow the headlines in the newspapers, the gossip or the criticism of others to upset you or bring about mental depression? If you do, you must admit you that are the cause of your own mood. You created your emotional reaction. Your attitude is wrong.

Do you imagine evil of others? If you do, notice the emotion generated in your deeper self; it is negative and destructive to your health and prosperity. Circumstances can affect you only as you permit them. You can voluntarily and definitely change your attitude toward life and all things. You can become master of your fate and captain of your soul (subconscious mind). Through disciplined, directed as well as controlled imagination, you can dominate and master your emotions and mental attitude in general.

If you imagine, for example, that another person is mean, dishonest and jealous, notice the emotion you evoked within yourself. Now reverse the situation. Begin to imagine the same person as honest, sincere, loving, also kind; notice the reaction it calls forth in you. Are you not, therefore, master of your attitudes?

In reality, the truth of the whole matter is that it is your real concept of God that determines your whole attitude toward life in general. Your dominant idea about God is your idea of life, for God is life. If you have the dominant idea or attitude that God is the Spiritual Power within you responsive to your thought and that, therefore, since your habitual thinking is constructive and harmonious, this Power is guiding and prospering you in all ways, this dominant attitude will color everything. You will be looking at the world through the positive, affirmative attitude of mind. Your outlook will be positive plus you will have a joyous expectancy of only the best.

Many people have a gloomy, despondent outlook on life. They are sour, cynical as well as cantankerous. This is due to the dominant negative mental attitude that directs their reaction to everything.

A young boy of sixteen going to high school said to me, 'I am getting very poor grades. My memory is failing. I do not know what's the matter?' The only thing wrong was his attitude. He adopted a new mental attitude by realizing how important his studies were in gaining entrance grades to college in order to become a lawyer. He began to pray scientifically, which is one of the quickest ways to change the mentality.

In scientific prayer, we deal with a principle that responds to thought. This young man realized that there was a Spiritual Power within him. Actually, that It was the only Cause and Power. Furthermore, he began to claim that his memory was perfect and that Infinite Intelligence constantly revealed to him everything he needed to know at all times, everywhere. He began to radiate love and goodwill to the teachers and fellow students. This young man is now enjoying a greater freedom than he had known for several years. He constantly imagines the teachers and his mother congratulating him on straight A-s. It is imagining the desired results that have followed this change of attitude toward his studies.

We have said previously that all our mental attitudes are conditioned by imagination. If you imagine that it is going to be a black day today, that business is going to be very poor, that it is raining, that no customers will come into your store, that they have no money and so on, you will experience the result of your negative imagery.

One time a man was walking the streets of London when he imagined he saw a snake on the street. Fear caused him to become semi-paralyzed. What he saw *looked* like a snake, but he had the same mental and emotional reaction as if it were a snake.

Imagine whatsoever things are lovely, noble and of good report. Your entire emotional attitude toward life will change. What do you imagine about life? Is it going to be a happy life for you? Or is it one long series of frustrations? 'Choose ye whom ye will serve.'

You mold, fashion and shape your outer world of experience according to the mental images you habitually dwell on. Imagine conditions and circumstances in life that dignify, elevate, please as well as satisfy you. If you imagine that life is cold, cruel, hard, bitter or that struggle and pain are inevitable, you are making life miserable for yourself.

Imagine yourself on the golf course. You are free, relaxed—full of enthusiasm and energy. Your joy is in overcoming all the difficulties presented by the golf course. The thrill is in surmounting all the obstacles.

Now let us take this scene: Imagine yourself going into a funeral parlor. Notice the different emotional response brought forward as you picture yourself in each of the above-mentioned situations. In the funeral chapel, you can rejoice in the person's new birthday. You can imagine the loved one surrounded by his or her friends in the midst of indescribable beauty and love. You can imagine God's river of peace flooding the minds and hearts of all present. You can actually ascend the heavens of your own mind wherever you are; this is the power of your imagination.

'And he dreamed yet another dream and told it his brethren and said, "Behold, I have dreamed a dream more; and behold, the sun and the moon and the eleven stars made obeisance to me."'

In ancient symbology, the sun and the moon represent the conscious and subconscious mind. The eleven stars represent the eleven powers in addition to imagination. Here again, the inspired writers are telling you that disciplined imagination takes precedence over all other faculties of the mind and controls the direction of the conscious and subconscious mind. Imagination is first and foremost; it can be scientifically directed.

I was examining one of the Round Towers of Ireland with my father over fifty years ago. He said nothing for one hour, but remained passive and receptive, seeming to be in a pensive mood. I asked him what he was meditating on. This is the essence of his answer: He pointed out that it is only by dwelling on the great, wonderful ideas of the world that we grow and expand. He contemplated the age of the stones in the tower, then his imagination took him back to the quarries where stones were first formed. His imagination unclothed the stones. He saw with the interior eye the structure, the geological formation, the composition of the stone and reduced it to the formless state; finally, he imagined the oneness of the stones with all stones and with all life. He realized in his Divine imagery that it was possible to reconstruct the history of the Irish race from looking at the Round Tower!

Through the imaginative faculty, this teacher was able to see the invisible men living in the Tower and to hear their voices. The whole place became alive to him in his imagination. Through this power, he was able to go back in time when there was no Round Tower there. In his mind, he began to weave a drama of the place from which stones originated, who brought them, the purpose of the structure as also the history connected with it. As he said to me, 'I am able to almost feel the touch and hear the sound, of steps that vanished thousands of years ago.'

The subjective mind permeates all things; it is in all things—is the substance from which they are made. The treasure house of eternity is in the very stones comprising a building. There is nothing inanimate; all is life in its varied manifestations. (The sun and the moon make obeisance to Joseph—imagination.) Truly through your faculty of imagination you can imagine that the invisible secrets of nature are revealed to you; you will find that you can delve the very depths of consciousness, calling things that be not as though they were and the unseen becomes seen.

The other night I sat in a park to look at the setting sun. Suddenly I began to think that the sun is like a house in the city of Los Angeles; there is a greater sun behind our sun-so on to infinity. It staggers the imagination to ponder and meditate on the myriads of suns and solar galaxies extending into infinity beyond the milky way. This world is only a grain of sand in the infinite seashore. Instead of seeing the parts, let us look at the wholeness, the unity of all things. We are, as the poet said, 'All parts of one stupendous whole, whose body nature is and God the soul.'

It is really out of the imaginative mind of man that all religions are born. Is it not out of the realm of imagination that television, radio, radar, super jets and all other modern inventions came? Your imagination is the treasure house of infinity, which releases to you all the precious jewels of music, art, poetry and inventions. You can look at some ancient ruin, an old temple or pyramid and reconstruct the records of the dead past. In the ruins of an old church yard, you can also see a modern city resurrected in all its beauty and glory. You may be in a prison of want, lack or behind stone bars, but in your imagination you can find an undreamed of measure of freedom.

Remember how Chico, the Parisian sewer cleaner, imagined and lived in a paradisaical state of mind called the seventh heaven even though he never saw the light of day?

Bunyan, in prison, wrote the great masterpiece *Pilgrim's Progress*. Milton, although blind, saw with the interior eye. His imagination made his brain a ball of fire and he wrote *Paradise Lost*. In this way he brought some of God's paradise to all people everywhere.

Imagination was Milton's spiritual eye, which enabled him to go about God's business whereby he annihilated time, space and matter and brought forth the truths of the Invisible Presence and Power.

A genius is a man who is in rapport with his subconscious mind. He is able to tap this universal reservoir and receive answers to his problems; thus, he does not have to work by the sweat of his brow. In the genius type of mind, the imaginative faculty is developed to a very high degree. All great poets and writers are gifted with a highly developed and cultivated imaginative faculty.

I can now see Shakespeare listening to the old stories, fables and myths of his day. I can also imagine him sitting down listing all these characters in the play in his mind ...then clothing them one by one with hair, skin, muscle and bone; animating them;

and making them so much alive that we think we are reading about ourselves.

Use your imagination and go about your Father's business. *Your Father's business* is to let your wisdom, skill, knowledge and ability come forth and bless others as well as yourself. You are about your Father's business if you are operating a small store and in your imagination you feel you are operating a larger store giving a greater measure of service to your fellow creature.

If you are a writer of short stories, you can be about your Father's business. Create a story in your mind that teaches something about the golden rule, then pass that story and all its characters through your spiritualized and highly artistic mentality; your article will be fascinating and intensely interesting to your public.

The truth about man is always wonderful and beautiful. When writing a novel or story, we should be sure that we clothe Truth in her garment of loveliness and beauty. You could now look at an acorn and with your imaginative eye construct a magnificent forest full of rivers, rivulets and streams. You could people the forest with all kinds of life; furthermore, you could hang a bow on every cloud. You could look at a desert and cause it to rejoice and blossom as a rose. "Instead of the thorn shall come up the fir tree and instead of the briar shall come up the myrtle tree.' Men gifted with intuition and imagination find water in the desert and they create cities where formerly other men only saw a desert and a wilderness.

An architect of a city sees the buildings and fountains already in operation before he ever digs a well or builds a house. 'I will make the wilderness a pool of water and the dry land springs of water?

Long hours, hard labor or burning the midnight oil will not produce a Milton, a Shakespeare or a Beethoven. People accomplish great things through quiet moments, imagining that the invisible things from the foundation of time are clearly visible.

You can imagine the indescribable beauty of He Who Is being expressed on your canvas and if you are a real artist in love with beauty, great beauty will come forth effortlessly. Moments of great inspiration will come to you; it will have nothing to do with perspiration or hard, mental labor.

In Greenwich Village, I met a poet who wrote beautiful poems; he had them printed on cards and sold them at Christmastime. Some of these poems were beautiful gems of spiritual love. He said that when he got still, the words would come into his mind accompanied by a lovely scene. Flowers, people and friends would come clearly into his mind. These images spoke to him. They told him their story. Oftentimes the entire poem, song or lullaby would appear complete and ready in his mind without the slightest effort. His habit was to imagine that he was writing beautiful poems that would stir the hearts of men.

Shelley said that poetry was an expression of the imagination. When the poet meditates on love and wishes to write on love, the Invisible Intelligence and Wisdom within him stirs his mind, casts the spell of God's beauty over him and awakens him to God's Eternal Love so that his words become clothed with wisdom, truth and beauty.

The Great Musician is within. If it is your business to play music or compose music, be sure that you are on your Father's Business. Your *Father's Business* is first of all to recognize God as the Great Musician. Then meditate, feel, pray to know that the Inner Music sings or plays through you—the Song of God's Love.. You will play like you have never played before.

Every invention of Edison's was first conceived in his imagination. The same was true of Tesla, another great inventor and scientist.

I think it was Oliver Wendell Holmes who said that we need three story spinners who can idealize, imagine as well as predict. I believe it was the capacity to imagine and dream that caused Ford to look forward to putting the world on wheels.

Your capacity to imagine causes you and enables you, to remove all barriers of time and space. You can reconstruct the past or contemplate the future thought through your inner eye. No wonder it says in Genesis: 'Israel loved Joseph [imagination] more than all his brethren. Imagination, when disciplined, spiritualized, controlled and directed becomes the most exalted and noblest attribute of man.

I was in a conversation some years ago with a young chemist who stated that his superiors for years had tried to manufacture a certain German dye and failed. He was given the assignment when he went with them. As he commented, he did not know that it could not be done and synthesized the compound without any difficulty. They were amazed and wanted to know his secret. His answer was that he imagined he had the answer. Pressed further by his superiors, he said that he could clearly see the letters 'Answer!' in blazing red color in his mind. He then created a vacuum underneath the letters, knowing that as he imagined the chemical formula underneath the letters, the subconscious would fill it in. The third night he had a dream in which the complete formula and the technique of making the compound was clearly presented.

'Joseph [imagination) is a dreamer and a dreamer of dreams.' 'They conspired against him to slay him. And they said one to another, Behold, this dreamer cometh.' Perhaps as you read these Biblical quotations there are thoughts of fear, doubt and anxiety conspiring in your own mind to slay or kill that desire, ideal or dream of yours. You look at conditions or circumstances and fear arises in your mind; yet there is the desire within you which, if realized, would bring you peace and solve your problem.

You must be like Joseph and become a practical dreamer. Decide to make your dreams come true. Withdraw and abstract your attention now from appearances of things and from sense evidence. Even though your senses deny what you pray for, affirm that it is true in your heart. Bring your mind back from its wandering after the false Gods of fear and doubt, to rest in the Omnipotence of the Spiritual Power within you. In the silence and quietude of your own mind, dwell on the fact that there is only One Power and One Presence. This Power and Presence is now responding to your thought as guidance, strength, peace and nourishment for the soul. Give all your mental attention to recognizing the absolute sovereignty of the Spiritual Power, knowing that the God-Power has the answer and is now showing you the way. Trust It, believe in It and walk the earth in the Light your prayer is already answered.

All of us read the story of Columbus and his discovery of America. It was imagination that led him to his discovery. His imagination plus faith in a Divine Power led him on and brought him to victory.

The sailors said to Columbus, 'What shall we do when all hope is gone?' His reply was, "You shall say at break of day, 'sail on, sail on and on. Here is the key to prayer; be faithful to the end; full of faith every step of the way, persisting to the end, knowing in your heart that the end is secure because you saw the end.

Copernicus through his vivid imagination revealed how the earth revolved on its axis, causing the old astronomical theories to be cast in the discard.

I think it would be a wonderful idea if all of us from time to time recast our ideas, checked up on our beliefs and opinions and asked ourselves honestly, 'Why do I believe that? Where did that opinion come from?' Perhaps many ideas, theories, beliefs and opinions that we hold are completely erroneous and were accepted by us as true without any investigation whatever as to their truth or accuracy. Because our father and grandfather believed in a certain way is no reason why we should.

One woman said to me that a certain idea she had must be true because her grandmother believed it. That is absurd! The race mind believes in many things that aren't true. What came down from generation to generation is not necessarily valid or the final word and authority.

The above-mentioned woman who was honest and well-meaning had a mind that was very touchy on psychological truths. She took everything in the Bible literally. This mind worked by prejudice, superstition and opposed everything that was not in accord with her established beliefs, opinions and preconceived notions.

Our mind must be like a parachute. The latter opens up; if it does not, it isn't any good. Likewise, we must open our eyes and minds to new truths. We must hunger and thirst after new truth and new knowledge, enabling us to soar aloft above our problems on the wings of faith and understanding.

The famous biologists, physicists, astronomers and mathematicians of our day are men gifted with a vivid, scientific imagination. For instance, the Einstein theory of relativity existed first in his imagination.

Archeologists and paleontologists studying the tombs of ancient Egypt through their imaginative perception reconstruct ancient scenes. The dead past becomes alive and audible once more. Looking at the ancient ruins and the hieroglyphics thereon, the scientist tells us of an age when there was no language. Communication was done by grunts, groans or signs. The scientist's imagination enables him to clothe this ancient temple with roofs; indeed, surround them with gardens, pools and fountains. The fossil remains are clothed with eyes, sinews and muscles. They again walk and talk. The past becomes the living present. We find actually in imagination that there is no time or space. Through your imaginative faculty, you can be a companion of the most inspired writers of all time.

Recently, I gave a lecture to our Sunday audience on the 21st chapter of Revelation in the Wilshire Ebell Theater in Los Angeles. The previous night while I was meditating on the inner meaning of the following verses, I intuitively and actually felt the presence and the intimate companionship of the mystic seer who wrote the inspired verses.

'And I John saw the holy city, new Jerusalem, coming down from God out of heaven, prepared as a bride adorned for her husband. And I heard a great voice out of heaven saying, 'Behold, the tabernacle of God is with men and he will dwell with them and be their God.' (Revelation 21:2, 2)

Now can't you walk down the corridor of your own mind to see, inwardly perceive, feel and sense God's river of peace flowing through your mind? You are now in the Holy City—your own mind—inhabited by such lovely people as bliss, joy, faith, harmony, love and goodwill. Your mind is clothed with God's radiant beauty; and your mood is exalted, noble and Godlike. You are married mentally and spiritually to God and to all things good. You have on your wedding garment, because you are in tune with the Infinite and God's Eternal Verities constantly impregnate your mind. In your imagination, you sense and feel that you are the tabernacle of God. You know that His Holy Spirit saturates and fills every part of your being. Your imagination now becomes seized with a Divine frenzy. You become God-intoxicated, having received the Divine antibody, the Presence of God in the chamber of your heart.

You can look at a rock. Out of that rock through Divine Imagination you can reveal the Madonna to portray a vision of beauty and a joy forever. Never permit your imagination to be used negatively; never distort or twist it. You can imagine sickness, accident and loss to allow yourself to become a mental wreck. To imagine sickness and lack is to destroy your peace of mind, health and happiness.

On board ship one time I heard a passenger exclaim when looking at the setting sun, 'I am so happy, I hope this lasts forever!'

How often have you seen a glorious sunrise-perhaps you said, 'I hope this lasts forever? Nothing in this transitory world lasts eternally; however, the Truths of God last forever. Darkness follows night, but morning will come again. Twilight will also come. You do not want things to stand still. You do not want to stand still either, for there are new worlds within and without to conquer. Change eternal is at the root of all life.

You do not want to remain in a rut. Problems are life's way of asking you for an answer. The greatest joy and satisfaction is in overcoming, in conquering. Life would become unbearable and unendurable if we did not experience change. We would be bored by the monotony of things. You meet with night and day, cold and heat, ebb and flow, summer and winter, hope and despair, success and failure. You find yourself moving through opposites; through your power to imagine what you wish and to feel its reality subjectively is to reconcile the opposites and bring peace to the mind.

In the midst of sorrow, grief or the loss of a loved one, your imagination and faith—the two wings of the bird—take you aloft into the very Bosom of God, your Father, where you find peace, solace and Divine rest for your soul.

In your imagination, you look into the very Face or Truth of God. Then God wipes away all tears—there shall be no more crying. All the mist or fog of the human mind dissolves in the sunshine of God's Love.

'And God shall wipe away all tears from their eyes; and there shall be no more death, neither sorrow, nor crying; neither, shall there be any more pain: for the former things are passed away. Behold I make all things new.' (Revelation 4, 5.)

When the night is black, you see no way out; that is, when your problem is most acute, let your imagination be your savior.

'I will lift up mine eyes [imagination) unto the hills, from whence cometh my help? (Psalm 121: 1.) *The hills* are of an inner range—the Presence of God in you. When you seek guidance and inspiration, fix your eyes on the stars of God's Truth, such as

'Infinite Intelligence leads and guides me,' or 'Divine Wisdom floods my mind and I am inspired from on High.'

There is a designer, an architect and a weaver within you; it takes the fabric of your mind, your thoughts, feelings and beliefs; and molds them into a pattern of life that brings you peace or discord, health or sickness. You can imagine a life that will take you up to the third heaven, where you will see unspeakable and unutterable things of God; or through the distorted, morbid use of your imagination you can sink to the depths of degradation.

Man is the tabernacle of God. No matter how low a man has sunk, the Healing Presence is there waiting to minister to him. It is within us waiting for us to call upon It. You can use your imagination in all business transactions in a wonderful way. Always imagine yourself in the other fellow's place; this tells you what to do. Imagine that the other is expressing all that you long to see him express. See him as he ought to be, not as he appears to be. Perhaps he is surly, sarcastic, bitter or hostile; there may be many frustrated hopes and tragedies lurking in his mind. Imagine whatsoever things are lovely and of good report and through your imagination you have covered him with the garment of God. God's world of ideals and God's infinite ideas are within him, waiting to be born and released. You can say if you wish, 'God waits to be born in him' You can open the door and kindle the fire of God's Love in that man's heart and perhaps the spark you lit will burst into a Divine Fire.

The greatest and richest galleries of art in the world are the galleries of the mind devoted to God's Truths and Beauty. Leonardo Da Vinci, through his gift of imagination, meditated on Jesus and the Twelve Disciples and what they meant. Lost in deep reverie, his imagination secreted the perfect pictures from the Infinite Reservoir within him. Due to his perfect focus his inner eye glowed with an interior luminosity, so that he was inspired-out of his Divine Imagery came the masterpiece: *The Last Supper*.

You have visited a quiet lake or a mountaintop. Notice how the placid, cool, calm surface reflected the heavenly lights, so does the quiet mind of the spiritual man reflect God's interior Lights and Wisdom.

Picture your ideal in life; live with this ideal. Let the ideal captivate your imagination; let the ideal thrill you! You will move in the direction of the ideal that governs your mind. The ideals of life are like the dew of heaven that move over the arid areas of man's mind, refreshing and invigorating him.

The inspired writer's imagination was fired with Truth when he wrote:

> *There is a river the streams whereof shall make glad the city of God, the holy place of the tabernacles of the most High. - Psalm 46:4.*

By now you know that imagination is the river enabling *you* to flow back psychologically to God. The streams and rivulets are your ideas and feelings, plus the emanation of love and goodwill that goes forth from you to all men everywhere. Man looks out into the world; and he sees sickness, chaos and man's inhumanity to man. The man with the disciplined imagination soars above all appearances, discord, apparent evidence to sees the sublime principle of harmony. It operates through, in as also behind all things. He knows through his Divine imagery that there is an Everlasting Law of Righteousness behind all things, an Ever-Abiding Peace, a Boundless Love governing the entire Cosmos. These Truths surge through the heart. They are born of the eternal Truth which through the imagination pierces the outer veil to rest in the Divine meaning of the way it is in God and Heaven.

Imagination was the workshop of God that inspired the writer of the following matchless, spiritual gemswhich will go down through the corridor of time and live forever. For tender beauty and for Divine imagery, they are unsurpassed in dealing with the availability and Immanence of God's Presence:

> *For he shall give his angels charge over thee, to keep thee in all thy ways. -Psalm 91:11.*
>
> *If I take the wings of the morning and dwell in the uttermost parts of the sea; even there shall thy hand lead me and thy right hand shall hold me. -Psalm 139.*

Chapter Two
Using the Subconscious Mind In Business

==================================

Long before our Bible was published, ancient wisdom said, 'As a man imagines and feels, so does he become.' This ancient teaching is lost in the night of time; it is lost in antiquity.

The Bible states, 'As a man thinketh in his heart, so is he.'

Legend relates that many thousands of years ago the Chinese sages gathered together under the leadership of a great sage to discuss the fact that vast legends of brutal invaders were pillaging and plundering the land. The question to be resolved was: 'How shall we preserve the ancient wisdom from the destruction of the invaders?'

There were many suggestions: Some thought that the ancient scrolls and symbols should be buried in the Himalayan mountains. Others suggested that the wisdom be deposited in monasteries in Tibet. Still others pointed out that the sacred temples of India were the ideal places for the preservation of the wisdom of their God.

The chief sage was silent during the entire discussion; in fact, he went to sleep in the midst of their talk and snored loudly, much to their dismay! He awakened in a little while and said, "Tao (God) gave me the answer: it is this: 'We will order the great pictorial artists of China—men gifted with Divine imagination-[which is the workshop of God] and tell them what we wish to accomplish. We will initiate them into the mysteries of Truth. They will portray or depict in picture form, the great

Truths which shall be preserved for all time and for countless generations yet unborn. When they are finished with the dramatization of the great Truths, Powers, Qualities and Attributes of God through a series of picture cards, we will tell the world about a new game that has been originated. Men throughout the world for all time will use them as a game of chance, not knowing that through this simple device, they are preserving the sacred teaching for all generations."' This was the origin of our own deck of cards.

The ancient Chinese sage, according to the legend, added, 'If all the sacred writings were destroyed, they could again be resurrected at any time through the symbolic teachings and inner meanings of the various designs on the playing cards.'

Imagination clothes all ideas and gives them form. Through the Divine artistry of imagination, these artists clothed all these ideas with pictorial form. In the act of imagination, that which is hidden in your deeper self is made manifest. Through imagination, what exists in latency or is asleep within you is given form in your thoughts. We contemplate what previously had not been revealed.

Let us take some simple examples: When you were going to be married, you had vivid, realistic pictures in your mind. With your power of imagination, you saw the minister, rabbi or priest. You heard him pronounce the words; you saw the flowers, the church. You also heard the music. You imagined the ring on your finger to you travel through your imagination on your honeymoon to Niagara Falls or Europe. All this was performed by your imagination.

Likewise before graduation, you had a beautiful, scenic drama taking place in your mind; you had clothed all your ideas about graduation in form. You imagined the professor or the president of the college giving you your diploma. You saw all the students dressed in gowns. You heard your mother or father or your girl- or boyfriend congratulate you. You felt the embrace and the kiss; it was all real, dramatic, exciting and wonderful.

Images appeared freely in your mind as if from nowhere, but you know and must admit that there was and is an Internal Creator with Power to mold all these forms that you saw in your mind; and endow them with life, motion and voice. These images said to you, 'For you only we live!'

A young man said to me in the army before he was discharged, 'I see my mother clearly. I can now imagine her welcome. I see the old home. Father is smoking a pipe. My sister is feeding the dogs. I can see every mark and corner of that home. I can even hear their voices.'

Where do all these vivid pictures come from? Keats said that there is an ancestral wisdom in man. We can, if we wish, drink of that old wine of heaven.

The spirit or God in you is the real basis of imagination. Once in an examination in London, I did not know the answer to an important question. I got still and quiet to say over and over again slowly, meditating in a relaxed way, 'God reveals the answer!' In the meantime, I went on answering the other questions, which were easy.

We know that when you relax the conscious mind, the subjective wisdom rises to the fore. In a short while, the picture of the answer came clearly into my mind. It was there in words like a page of a book, with the entire answer written out as a graph in the mind. A Mightier Wisdom than that of my conscious mind or intellect spoke through me.

I had a very religious school boy about 14 years old come to me. Whenever he had a problem, he said to me that he would imagine Jesus was talking to him, giving him the answer to his problem and telling him what to do. His mother was very ill; this boy was highly imaginative. He read the story of Jesus healing the woman with fever. My little friend related to me, 'Last night I imagined Jesus saying to me, "Go thy way; thy mother is made whole!" He made that drama of the mind so real, vivid and intense, that due to his faith and belief, he convinced himself of the truth of what he heard subjectively.

His mother was completely healed, yet she was considered at that time hopeless and beyond medical help.

Being a student of the laws of mind, you know what happened. He galvanized himself into the feeling of being one with his image and according to his faith or conviction was it done unto him. There is only One Mind and One Healing Presence. As the boy changed his conviction about his mother and felt her perfect health, the idea of perfect health was resurrected in her mind simultaneously. He did not know anything about spiritual healing or the power of imagination. He operated the law unconsciously and believed in his own mind that Jesus was actually talking to him; then, according to his belief, was it done unto him.

To believe something is to accept it as true. This is why Paracelsus said in the 16th century, 'Whether the object of your belief be true or false, you will get the same results. There is only one spiritual, healing Principle and one Process of healing called *faith*. 'According to your faith is it done unto you.' There are many processes, methods as also techniques of healing. All of them get results—, not because of the particular technique or method, but because of imagination and faith in the particular process. They are all tapping the One Source of healing, which is God. The Infinite Healing Presence permeates all things and is omnipresent.

The voodoo doctor with his incantations gets results. So does the kahuna of Hawaii with his ministrations, the various branches of New Thought and Christian Science, the Nancy School of Medicine, osteopathy and so on. All these schools of thought are meeting levels of consciousness that are doing good.

Any method or process that alleviates human misery, pain and distress is good. Many churches practice the laying on of hands; others make novenas and visit shrines; all are benefited according to their mental acceptance or belief.

When you are willing to stand alone with God that is, to cease completely giving power to external things, when you no longer give power to the world of phenomena, which means to make a world of effect a cause. When all your allegiance is given to the Spiritual Power within you, realizing it as the only Presence and the only Cause, you will not need any props of any kind. The Living Intelligence that made your body will respond immediately to your faith and understanding; and you will have an instantaneous, spiritual healing. If you are not at that level of consciousness where you can grow a tooth through prayer, the obvious thing to do is to go see a dentist. Pray for him and for a perfect, Divine oral adjustment. As long as you believe in external causes, you will seek external remedies.

To illustrate further the power of imagination, I will tell you about a close relative of mine who had tuberculosis. His lungs were badly diseased, so his son decided to heal his father. He came home to Perth, Western Australia, where his father lived. He told his father that he had met a monk who sold him a piece of the true cross, which he had paid him the equivalent of $500 for it. (This young man had picked up a splinter of wood off the sidewalk, went to a jeweller's and had it set in a ring so that it looked real.) He told his father that many were healed just by touching the ring or the cross. He inflamed and fired his father's imagination to the point that the old gentleman snatched the ring from him, placed it over his chest, prayed silently and went to sleep. In the morning, he was healed; all the clinic's tests were negative.

You know, of course, that it was not the splinter of wood from the sidewalk that healed him. It was his imagination aroused to an intense degree, plus the confident expectancy of a perfect healing. Imagination was joined to faith or subjective feeling. The union of the two brought about the healing. The father never learned the trick that had been played upon him; if he had, he probably would have had a relapse. He remained completely cured and passed away 15 years later at the age of 89.

I know a businessman here in Los Angeles who has reached the top in his field. He told me that for thirty years the most important decisions he ever made were based on his imaginary conversations with Paul. I asked him to elaborate. He then remarked that few people in the business world realized the wonderful guidance and counsel they could receive by dramatizing in their imagination that they were receiving counsel from the writers or great seers of the Bible.

I will quote this successful executive as accurately as I can: 'Many times my decisions might have prospered the company or plunged it into bankruptcy. I vacillated, wavered, got high blood pressure and heart disease. One day the idea came to me: Why not ask Jesus or Paul? I loved the Epistles of Paul, so when an important decision was to be made, I would imagine Paul was saying to me: 'Your decision is perfect; it will bless your organization. Bless you, my son! Keep on God's path'. After imagining I saw Paul and heard him, a wave of peace and inner tranquility would seize me; I was at peace about all decisions.'

This was this businessman's way of receiving Divine Guidance by using his imagination to convince himself about the right action. There is only one Principle of Intelligence in this world; all that is really necessary is to say and believe, 'God is guiding me now and there is only right action in my life.'

The mind, as Troward tells you, works like a syllogism. If your premise is correct, the conclusion or result will correspond. The subjective reasons deductively only and its sequence or conclusion is always in harmony with the premise. Establish the right premise in your mind; you will be subjectively compelled to right action. Inner movement of the mind is action. The external movements and action is the automatic response of the body to the internal motion of the mind. Hearing a friend or associate congratulate you on your wonderful decision will induce the movement of right action in your life.

The man who used St Paul to impregnate his mind with the belief of right action was using the One Eternal Principle of Intelligence. His technique of arriving at that place in his mind does not really matter.

Goethe used his imagination wisely when confronted with difficulties and predicaments. His biographers point out that he was accustomed to filling many hours quietly holding imaginary conversations. It is well known that his custom was to imagine one of his friends before him in a chair answering in the right way. In other words, if he were concerned over any problems, he imagined that his friend was giving him the right or appropriate answer, accompanied with the usual gestures and tonal qualities of the voice, making the entire imaginary scene as real and vivid as possible.

I was very well acquainted with a stockbroker in New York City who used to attend my classes at Steinway Hall there. His method of solving financial difficulties was very simple. He would have mental, imaginary conversations with a multimillionaire banker-friend of his who used to congratulate him on his wise and sound judgment and compliment him on his purchase of the right stocks. He used to dramatize this imaginary conversation until he had psychologically fixed it as a form of belief in his mind.

Mr Nicols, Ouspensky's student, used to say, 'Watch your inner talking and let it agree with your aim.'

This broker's inner talking or speech certainly agreed with his aim to make sound investments for himself and his clients. He told me that his main purpose in his business life was to make money for others and to see them prosper financially by his wise counsel. It is quite obvious that he was using the laws of mind constructively.

Prayer is a habit. This broker regularly and at frequent intervals during the day returned to the mental image in his mind; he made it a deep, subjective pattern. That which is embodied subjectively is objectively expressed. It is the *sustained* mental picture that is developed in the dark house of the mind. Run your mental movie often. Get into the habit of flashing it on the screen of your mind frequently. After a while it will become a definite, habitual pattern. The inner movie that you have seen with your mind's eye shall be made manifest openly: 'He calleth things that be not as though they were and the unseen becomes seen.'

Many people solve their dilemmas and problems by the play of their imagination, knowing that whatever they imagine and feel as true, will and must come to pass.

Sometime ago, a certain young woman was involved in a complicated lawsuit that had persisted for five years. There was one postponement after another, with no solution in sight. At my suggestion, she began to dramatize as vividly as possible her lawyer having an animated discussion with her regarding the outcome. She would ask him questions. He would answer her appropriately; then she condensed the whole thing down to a simple phrase, as suggested years ago by the French School of Mental Therapeutics. She had him repeat it over and over again to her. The phrase she said was: 'There has been a perfect, harmonious solution. The whole case is settled outside court.'

She kept looking at the mental picture whenever she had a spare moment. While in a restaurant for a cup of coffee, she ran the mental movie with gestures, voice and sound equipment. She could imagine easily the sound of his voice, smile and mannerisms. She ran the movie so often that it became a subjective pattern-a regular train track. It was written in her mind; or as the Bible says, it was 'written in her heart and inscribed in her inward parts. Her conclusion was: 'It is God in action, "meaning all-around harmony and peace." (*Harmony* is of God and what you want in a legal case is a harmonious solution.)

In the science of imagination, you must first of all begin to discipline your imagination and not let it run riot. Science insists upon purity. If you wish a chemically pure product, you must remove all traces of other substances as well as extraneous material. You must, in other words, separate out and cast away all the dross.

In the science of imagination, you eliminate all the mental impurities, such as fear, worry, destructive inner talking, self-condemnation and the mental union with other miscellaneous negatives. You must focus all your attention on your ideal and refuse to be swerved from your purpose or aim in life. As you get mentally absorbed in the reality of your ideal, by loving and remaining faithful to it, you will see your desire take form in your world. In the book of Joshua it says, "Choose ye this day whom ye shall serve? Let your choice be, 'I am going to imagine whatsoever things are lovely and of good report.'

I know and have talked to many people who diabolically invert the use of their God-given faculty. The mother, for example, imagines that something bad has happened to her son, John, because he is late coming home. She imagines an accident, a hospital, Johnny in the operating room and so on.

A businessman whose affairs are prospering, yet dwells on negativity, is another example of the destructive use of imagination. He comes home from the office, runs a motion picture in his mind of failure, sees the shelves empty, imagines himself going into bankruptcy, an empty bank balance. The business closed down ...yet all the time he is actually prospering. There is no truth whatsoever in that negative mental picture of his; it is a lie made out of whole cloth. In other words, the thing he fears does not exist save in his morbid imagination; the failure will never come to pass, except he keeps up that morbid picture charged with the emotion of fear. If he constantly indulges in this mental picture, he will, of course, bring failure to pass. He had the choice of failure or success, but he chose failure.

There are chronic worriers; they never seem to imagine anything good or lovely. They seem to know that something bad or destructive is always going to happen. They cannot tell you one reason why something good should and could happen;

however, they are ready with all the reasons why something dire and evil should occur.

Why is this? The reason is simple: These people are habitually negative; that is, most of their thinking is of a negative, chaotic, destructive, morbid nature. As they continue to make a habit of these negative patterns of thought, they condition their subconscious mind negatively. Their imagination is governed by their dominant moods and feelings; this is why they imagine evil, even about their loved ones.

For example, if their son happens to be in the army, they imagine that he is going to catch cold, become an alcoholic, become loose morally; or if he is in combat, they imagine he will be shot—all manner of destructive images enter their mind. This is due to the hypnotic spell of habit. Their prayers are rendered null and void.

Make a choice now! Begin to think constructively and harmoniously. *To think* is to speak. Your thought is your word. Let your words be as a honeycomb, sweet to the ear and pleasant to the bones. Let your words be 'like apples of gold in pictures of silver. The future is the present grown up; it is your invisible word or thought made visible. Are your words sweet to the ear? What is your inner speech like at this moment? No one hear you; it is your own silent thought. Perhaps you are saying to yourself, 'I can't; it is impossible. 'I'm too old now. 'What chance have I?' 'Mary can, but I can't. I have no money. I can't afford this or that. I've tried; it's no use. You can see your words are not like a honeycomb. They are not sweet to your ear; they do not lift you up or inspire you.

Ouspensky was always stressing the importance of inner speech, inner conversation or inner talking. It is really the way you feel inside; for the inside mirrors the outside. Is your inner speech pleasant to the bones? Does it exalt you, thrill you or make you happy?

Bones are symbolic of support and symmetry. Let your inner talking sustain and strengthen you. 'But the word is very nigh unto thee, in thy mouth and in thy heart, that thou mayest do it. See, I have set before thee this day life and good and death and evil.'

Decree now to say it deliberately: 'From this moment forward, I will admit to my mind for mental consumption only those ideas and thoughts that heal, bless, inspire and strengthen me. Let your words from now on be as 'apples of gold in pictures of silver. An apple is a delicious fruit. Gold means 'power. *Pictures of silver* mean in the Bible 'your desires? The *picture* in your mind is the way you want things to be. It is the picture of your fulfilled desire. It could be a new position or health. Let your words, your inner silent thoughts—feelings coincide and agree with the *picture of silver* or your desire. Desire and feeling joined together in a mental marriage will become the answered prayer.

Be sure you follow the imagination of the Bible and let your words be sweet to the ear. What are you giving *your ear* to now? What are you listening to? What are you giving attention to? Whatever you give attention to will grow, magnify and multiply in your experience.

'Faith comes by hearing, Paul says. Listen to the great truths of God. Listen to the voice of God. What language does He speak in? It is not Gaelic, French or Italian; but the universal language or mood of love, peace, joy, harmony, faith, confidence as also goodwill. Give your ear to these qualities and potencies of God. Mentally eat of these qualities; and as you continue to do so, you will be conditioned to those positive, enduring qualities. The Law of Love will govern you.

You have heard this oft-repeated quotation, 'Man is made in the image and likeness of God? This means that your mind is God's mind, as there is only One Mind. Your Spirit is God's Spirit and you create in exactly the same way and through the same law as God creates. Your individual world; that is, experiences, conditions, circumstances, environment, as well as your physical health, financial states as well as social life, et cetera, is made out of your own mental images and after your own likeness.

Like attracts like. Your world is a mirror reflecting back to you your inner world of thought, feeling, beliefs and inner conversation. If you begin to imagine evil powers working against you or that there is a jinx following you or that other forces and people are working against you, there will be a response of your deeper mind to correspond with these negative pictures and fears in your mind. Consequently, you will begin to say that everything is against you or that the stars are opposed to you. Maybe you will blame karma, your past lives or some demon.

Truly the only sin is ignorance. Pain is not a punishment; it is the consequence of the misuse of your inner power. Come back to the one Truth to realize that there is only One Spiritual Power. It functions through the thoughts and images of your mind. The problems, vexations and strife are due to the fact that man has actually wandered away after false Gods of fear and error. He must return to the center—the God-Presence within. Affirm now the sovereignty and authority of this Spiritual Power within you—the Principle of all life. Claim Divine guidance, strength, nourishment, peace and this Power will respond accordingly.

I will now proceed to point out how you may definitely and positively convey an idea or mental image to your subconscious mind. The conscious mind of man is personal and selective. It chooses, selects, weighs, analyzes, dissects—just to investigate. It is capable of inductive and deductive reasoning. The subjective or subconscious mind is subject to the conscious mind. It might be called a servant of the conscious mind. The subconscious obeys the order of the conscious mind. Your conscious thought has power. The power you are acquainted with is thought. In the back of your thought is Mind, Spirit or God. Focused, directed thoughts reach the subjective levels;

they must be of a certain degree of intensity. Intensity is acquired by concentration.

To *concentrate* is to come back to the center and contemplate the Infinite Power within you that lies stretched in smiling repose. To concentrate properly, you still the wheels of your mind and enter into a quiet, relaxed mental state. When you concentrate, you gather your thoughts together to focus all your attention on your ideal, aim or objective. You are now at a focal or central point, where you are giving all your attention and devotion to your mental image. The procedure of focused attention is somewhat similar to that of a magnifying glass as it can focus on the rays of the sun. You can see the difference in the effect of scattered vibrations of the sun's heat as also the vibrations that emanate from a central point. You can direct the rays of the magnifying glass so that it will burn up a particular object upon which it is directed. Focused, steadied attention of your mental images gains a similar intensity; and a deep, lasting impression is made on the sensitive plate of the subconscious mind.

You may have to repeat this drama of the mind many times before you can make an impression. Yet the secret of impregnating the deeper mind is continuous or sustained imagination. When fear or worry comes to you during the day, you can always immediately gaze upon that lovely picture in your mind, realizing and knowing that you have operated a definite psychological law that is now working for you in the dark house of your mind. As you do so, you are truly watering the seed to fertilize it, by this means accelerating its growth.

The conscious mind of man is the motor; the subconscious is the engine. You must start the motor. The engine will do the work. The conscious mind is the dynamo that awakens the power of the subconscious.

The first step in conveying your clarified desire, idea or image to the deeper mind is to relax, immobilize the attention to get still and quiet. This quiet, relaxed, peaceful attitude of mind prevents extraneous matter and false ideas from interfering with your mental absorption of your ideal; furthermore, in the quiet, passive, receptive attitude of mind, effort is reduced to a minimum.

In the second step, you begin to imagine the reality of that which you desire. For example, you may wish to sell a home. In private consultation with real estate brokers, I have told them of the way I sold my own home; they have applied it with remarkable results. I placed a sign in the garden in front of my home that read: 'For sale by owner. The second day after placing the sign, I said to myself as I was going to sleep, 'supposing you sold the house, what would you do?'

I answered my own question as I said, 'I would take that sign down and throw it in the garage. In my imagination, I took hold of the sign, pulled it up from the ground, placed it on my shoulders, went to the garage to toss it on the floor, saying jokingly to the sign, 'I don't need you anymore!' I felt the inner satisfaction of it all, realizing that it was finished. The next day a man gave me a deposit of $1,000 and said, 'Take your sign down; we will go into escrow now.'

Immediately I pulled the sign up and took it into the garage. The outer action conformed to the inner. There is nothing new about this. 'As within, so without' meaning according to the image impressed on the subconscious mind, so is it on the objective screen of your life.

This procedure or technique is older than our Bible. The outside mirrors the inside. External action follows internal action.

I was engaged by a very large organization to do some spiritual work for them. Through fraudulent means, others tried to lay claim to their vast mining and other interests. They harassed the company by legal trickery—just to try to get something for nothing. I told the lawyer to dramatize vividly in his imagination several times daily the president of the company that he represented congratulating him on the perfect, harmonious solution. As he sustained the mental picture, through continuous, mental application, the subjective wisdom gave him some new ideas—as he said, 'Right out of the blue!' He followed these up. The case was closed soon afterward.

If a person has a mortgage due at the bank but he does not have the money to cover it, if he will faithfully apply this principle, the subconscious mind will provide him with the money. Never mind, how, when, where or through what source? The subjective mind has ways you know not of; its ways are past finding out. It is one of the instruments or tools that God gave man, so he could provide himself with all things necessary for his welfare. The man who hasn't the money to meet the mortgage can imagine himself depositing a check or currency required in the bank; that is, giving it to the cashier. The important point is to become intensely interested in the mental picture or imaginary act, making it real and natural. The more earnestly he engages his mind on the imaginary drama, the more effectually will the imaginary act be deposited in the bank of the subconscious mind. You can take a trip to the teller's window in your imagination. Make it so real and true that it will actually take place physically.

There is a young lady who comes to our Sundaymorning lectures regularly. She had to change buses three times; it took her one and one half hours each Sunday to come to the lectures. In the sermon, I told how a young man prayed for a car and received one. She went home and experimented as follows: Here is her letter, in part, published by her permission:

> *Dear Dr Murphy:*
>
> *This is how I received a Cadillac [sic]; I wanted one to come to the lectures on Sunday and Tuesdays. In my imagination I went through the identical process I would go through if I were actually driving a car. I went to the show room. The salesman took me for a ride in one. I also drove it several blocks. I claimed the Cadillac car as my own over and over again. I kept the mental picture of getting into the car, driving it, feeling the upholstery,*

etc., consistently for over two weeks. Last Sunday I drove to your meeting in a Cadillac. My uncle in Inglewood passed away; left me his Cadillac and his entire estate.

If you are saying, well, I do not know of any way to get the money to pay off the mortgage, do not worry about it. To worry means to strangle. Realize that there is a Power inherent within you that can provide you with everything you need when you call upon It. You can decree now with feeling and conviction: 'My house is free from all debt and wealth flows to me in avalanches of abundance. Do not question the manner in which the answer to your prayer will come. You will do the obvious things necessary, knowing that the subconscious intelligence is directing all your steps, for it knows everything necessary for the fulfillment of your desires. You can also imagine a letter from the mortgage company informing you that you are paid up; rejoice in that image. Live with that imaginary letter in your mind until it becomes a conviction.

Become convinced now that there is a power within you that is capable of bringing what you imagine and feel as true into manifestation. Sitting idly by, daydreaming or just imagining the things you would like to possess will not attract them to you. You must know, actually believe that you are operating a law of mind. Be convinced of your God-given power to use your mind constructively to bring the thing you desire into reality.

Know what you want. The subconscious mind will carry out the idea, because you have a definite, clear-cut concept of what you wish to possess. Imagine clearly the fulfillment of your desire; then you are giving the subconscious something definite to act upon. The subconscious mind is the film upon which the picture is impressed. The subconscious develops the picture; and sends it back to you in a material, objectified form.

The camera is *you* consciously imagining the realization of your desire through focused attention. As you do this in a relaxed, happy mood, the picture is cast on the sensitive film of the subconscious mind. You also need a time exposure; it may be two or three minutes or longer depending on your temperament, feeling and understanding. The important thing to remember is that it is not so much the time as the quality of your consciousness, degree of feeling or faith. Generally speaking, the more focused and absorbed your attention and the longer the time, the more perfect will be the answer to your prayer. *Believe* that you have received and ye shall receive. "Whatsoever ye shall ask in prayer, believing, ye shall receive.' *To believe* is to accept something as true or to live in the state of being it; as you sustain this mood, you shall experience the joy of the answered prayer!

Chapter Three
How to Imagine Success

==============================

God is always successful in His undertakings. Man is equipped to succeed because God is within him. All the attributes, qualities and potencies of God are within.

You were born to win, to conquer indeed, to overcome! The Intelligence, Wisdom as well as Power of God are within you waiting to be released and enabling you to rise above all difficulties.

There are many men who quietly use the abstract term *Success*, over and over many times a day until they reach a conviction that success is theirs. Remember that the *idea of success* contains all the essential elements of success. As man repeats the word Success to himself with faith and conviction, his subconscious mind will accept it as true of himself. Now will be under subjective compulsion to succeed.

We are compelled to express not only our subjective beliefs, impressions but also convictions. The ideal way to succeed is to know what you want to achieve. If you do not know your right place or what you would like to do, you can ask for guidance on the question. The deeper mind will respond; as a result, you will find a push or tendency in a certain field of activity.

The deeper mind is responsive to your thought. The subconscious—sometimes called 'subjective or deeper mind, sets in operation its unconscious intelligence that attracts to the individual the conditions necessary for his success. Man should make it a special point to do the thing he loves to do. When you are happy in your endeavour, you are a success.

Accept the fact that you have an inner Creative Power. Let this be a positive conviction. This Infinite Power is responsive and reactive to your thought. To know, understand as also apply this principle makes doubt, fear and worry gradually disappear.

If a man dwells on the thought, for example, of failure, the thought of failure attracts failure. The subconscious takes the thought of failure as his request to proceed to make his experience the reality. Only because he indulges in the mental practice of conceiving failure. The subconscious mind is impersonal and nonselective.

A business friend of mine, a tailor by trade, has a favorite saying: 'All I ever do is add. I never subtract? He means that *success* is a plus sign. *Add* to your growth, wealth and power, knowledge, faith as well as wisdom.

Life is addition! Death is subtraction. You add to your life by imagining whatsoever things are true, lovely, noble as also Godlike. Imagine and feel yourself successful. You must become successful. You arc never a slave to circumstances, environment or conditions. You are master of conditions. You can become a victim of conditions by mentally acquiescing to the present state of things. As you change your mind, you change conditions.

A movie actor told me once that he had very little education, but he had a dream as a boy of bring a successful movie actor. Out in the field mowing hay or driving the cows home or even when milking them, he said, 'I would constantly imagine that I saw my name in big lights in a large theater. I kept this up for years until finally I ran away from home; got extra jobs in the motion picture field; and the day came when I saw my name in great big lights, as I did when I was a boy! Then he added, 'I know the power of *sustained* imagination to bring success.'

What does *success* imply to you? You want undoubtedly to be successful in your relationship with others. You wish to be outstanding in your chosen work or profession. You wish to possess a beautiful home with all the money you need to live comfortably and happily. You want to be successful in your prayers to be in your contact with the Universal Power within you.

Imagine yourself doing the things you long to doactually possessing the things you long to possess. Become imaginative; mentally participate in the reality of the successful state; enter into that state of consciousness frequently; make a habit of it; then you will find you will be guided to do everything necessary for the realization of your dream. Go to sleep feeling successful every night and perfectly satisfied. You will succeed eventually in implanting the idea of success in your subconscious mind.

I know a drug clerk who was a licensed pharmacist receiving $40 a week plus his commission on sales. After 25 years, he told me, 'I will get a pension and retire.'

I said to him, "Why don't you own your own store? Get out of this place. Raise your sights! Have a dream for your children. Maybe your son wants to be a doctor or your daughter desires to be a musician.'

His answer was that he had no money! He began to awaken to the fact that whatever he could conceive as true, he could give it conception.

The first step toward your goal is the *birth of the idea* in the mind. The second step is the *manifestation of the idea*. He began to imagine that he was in his own store. He participated in the act mentally. He arranged the bottles, dispensed prescriptions as also imagined several clerks in the store waiting on customers. He visualized a big bank balance. Mentally he worked in that imaginary store. Like a good actor, he lived the role. (Act as though I am and I will be.) This drugstore clerk put himself wholeheartedly into the act ... living, moving essentially acting in the assumption that his store was his.

The sequel was interesting. He was discharged from his position, went with a large chain store, became manager and then district manager. He made enough money in four years to make a down payment on a drugstore of his own. He called it his 'dream pharmacy.' 'It was', he said, 'exactly the store he saw in his imagination.' He became successful in his chosen field and was happy doing what he loved to do.

The individual who habitually maintains a mental attitude of faith and expectancy of the best is bound to succeed and advance in life. The individual who is depressed, dejected, morbid and despondent attracts failure all along the line. Fear is truly a lack of faith in Divine supply. It is faith misplaced. Fear is faith in the wrong thing. Fear is a belief in lack or that man's good is being withheld from him.

'Son, thou are ever with me and all that I hath is thine.' All things you need are in the invisible. It could be said that all things needed are in the abstract. You must desire to be greater than you are, in order to advance in life. Desire comes first, followed by a recognition of the Power within you enabling you to manifest what you want. The subconscious mind is the medium through which all that you desire can be brought into objectivity. You are the one giving orders in the form of habitual thinking, feeling, opinions and beliefs. The subconscious mind obeys the orders given by the conscious mind. If your conscious mind is opposed to all negative thoughts, they can make no impression upon your subconscious mind. You become immunized.

If, for example, you say, 'I wish I were healthy, then I could be much more successful in my work;' begin *now* to realize that your body is your mind expressed. The subconscious mind is the builder of the body and controls all its vital functions. Your conscious mind has the power to change any idea or group of thoughts held in the subconscious mind. You can impress the idea of health on your subconscious mind when you know that it can be done. A conviction and sincere belief is necessary. Affirmative statements establish definite impression on the subconscious mind.

A wonderful way to impress the subconscious is through disciplined or scientific imagination. By illustration, if your knee is swollen and you are lame, imagine that you're doing the things you would do if you were in perfect health. You might say that I would go downtown on a bus, visit friends, ride horseback, go swimming or hiking. First in your imagination you go on these psychological journeys, making them as real and natural as possible. *Continue* to go on these psychological journeys! You know that self-motivation is yours. All movement is first of the mind or consciousness of man before any external movement can take place.

By example, the chair does not move of itself. You must impart motion to it. The same is true of your body. As you continue to do all the things you would do were you healed, this inner movement will cause the subconscious to build the body in accordance with the image back of it.

The following is a wonderful prayer for perfect health. A minister I knew in South Africa applied this prayer and healed himself. Several times a day he would affirm slowly and quietly, first making certain that he was completely relaxed mentally and physically: "The perfection of God is now being expressed through me. The idea of health is now filling my subconscious mind. The image that God has of me is a perfect image. My subconscious mind re-creates my body in perfect accordance with the perfect image held in the mind of God. This is a simple, easy way of conveying the idea of perfect health to your subconscious mind.

You can develop confidence by knowing and realizing that nothing can prevent you from achieving success. Develop a certainty in your mind that this Inner Power can be called upon to overcome all obstacles. There must be an assurance and determination on your part that you can achieve and accomplish what you set out to do. This positive, affirmative attitude constitutes confidence.

You have heard the Biblical expression: According to your faith is it done unto you. Faith in God is the realization that there is only One Spiritual Power that is Omnipresent, Omniscient, Omnipotent, All Love, All Light, All Beauty, All Life with An Ever-Present Help in time of trouble. Know that His Power responds to your thought.

Cease looking upon God as some Being living in the skies with a long beard. God is the Essence of man. God is the Life of man. We cannot comprehend all of God, for the finite mind cannot comprehend the Infinite en toto.

For example, your conscious and subconscious mind are projections of God; they are working tools. God is Infinite Wisdom, Boundless Love and Infinite Intelligence along with Absolute Bliss, Eternal Harmony and Indescribable Beauty. All these and others, are Qualities and Attributes of God.

You are not cast adrift on the ocean of life deserted by the Creator of Life. This Presence and Power is within you. This Knowledge or Awareness of Divinity within you is the greatest and most powerful contributing factor to success.

Develop your talents; begin to use them; they are God-given. You have faculties and powers which require constant development.

'Man shall decree a thing and it shall come to pass.' What are you mentally decreeing now? What is the nature of your inner talking, inner conversation as also your idle moods? Man shall account for every idle word he speaks. The idle words are doubt, fear, anxiety plus worry. If these are present, you are not giving definite, positive orders to your subconscious mind, because there is no definite impression made as to what you wish to bring to pass.

Fear and worry cause confusion in the conscious mind. This creates confusion in the subconscious mind and nothing happens but confusion in man's affairs. Continue to trust in the

Divine Power and that which you desire will come to you in some manner. Have faith in God, in the Divine Power, in His Divine Love and His Overshadowing Presence always watching over you and you will become invincible. 'Trust in the Lord and do good; *so* shalt thou dwell in the land and verily thou shalt be fed'